Narrative Design for Indies:

GETTING STARTED

Edwin McRae

Contents

Yes, this blank page is here for you to write on. Please...make notes!

1

Why is Narrative Design different for Indies?

Money, money and...money.

You either can't afford to tell a AAA fidelity story or you have a different motive other than making great swags of cash, like raising awareness, making people think or generally improving the human condition.

Regardless of your motives, I'm genuinely sorry to say that story is expensive.

That leaves us with a bit of a conundrum, doesn't it? How do you afford to hire an experienced narrative designer on an Indie budget? Actually, that's an easy one. If you only need that writer for an hour or six then no problem. If you have a 200,000 word JRPG epic to produce then you're arguably *not* making an Indie game.

The question is not really how you can afford a writer. The question is really...how much do you *need* a writer?

That's what this book is about. Helping you work out what your story demands will be *before* you bring a writer in to make them happen. Because here's the thing...much of my freelancing career has been spent working with Indie game developers, asking them lots of tricky questions in order to establish exactly how they are going to tell their story within the limited means they have available.

I'm not complaining. I enjoy that sort of thing. In fact, it's pretty awesome to be able to help someone finally express the narrative that's been festering within for umpteen years. But it's hard not to feel bad about getting paid to tell people things that they *should already know*. And most of the time they *do* actually know it. They just haven't thought about it in the right way, mainly because they haven't had the right questions to ask or haven't been aware of the narrative tools at their disposal.

So that's what's on offer here. The right questions. The right tools. The hammer and chisel with which to craft your story rather than the diamond-headed drills and high-powered laser cutters that you simply can't afford. Well, that's actually a tall order for a book of this modest magnitude. There are far more nifty things you can do with a hammer and chisel than we can hope to cover here. In the meantime, this little book will get you chipping away and hopefully save you a bunch of money in the process.

Save the narrative design budget for the important bit...making your story happen. For now, and for the price of a Big Mac combo, let's see if we can help you tell your Game Story within the means of Indie game development.

2

Plot vs Story

What's the difference?

There's one *massive* pitfall that I've seen many an Indie dev tumble into, and it's wanting a story for their game but not knowing exactly what a story is. You see, every game needs a story, but not every game needs a plot. And trying to apply a plot to a game that only needs a story will land you in hot water, both mentally and financially.

Okay, so what's the difference between Plot and Story?

Plot is generally defined as 'the main events of a play, novel, film, or similar work (e.g. video game), devised and presented by the writer as an interrelated sequence'.

Narrative is 'a spoken or written account of connected events; a story'.

Story is 'an account of imaginary or real people and events told for entertainment' and also 'a plot or storyline'.

Which is all very bloody confusing!

So I'm going to lean on the wisdom of the great writer, E M Forster. To be honest, I've never read any of his work but I love his eloquent description of the plot/story conundrum.

> 'The king died and then the queen died' is a story. 'The king died, and then queen died of grief' is a plot.
>
> – E M Forster

ASPECTS OF THE NOVEL (1927)

'The king died and then the queen died.' Both are dramatic events but at the moment they're seemingly unconnected. Perhaps the king slipped in the shower and the queen was asphyxiated by an overzealous corset attendant. So these are two separate events that make up a 'story'. Stuff happens.

If the queen dies of a broken heart because she failed to buy that non-slip bathmat she'd had her eye on for weeks then we have 'plot', a clear causal connection between one event and the other. King dies. Queen blames herself for her beloved's demise and is overwhelmed with grief and guilt. She shuffles around in a tormented daze until blithely stepping in front of a runaway stagecoach.

A causes B.

Plot is the food and drink of film and television. The Hero's Journey and all that malarky? It's all plot structure, and those mediums have spent decades working out what a 'good plot' looks like. It's linear and every event is linked in some way. Events cause other events until we reach some sort of concluding event, like the rebels blow up the Death Star or the beloved northern English actor gets killed for the umpteenth time, which is all very fine and dandy when your audience is happily sitting there, soaking it all in.

But what happens when your audience wants to get involved? What if they want to take the plot in a totally different direction? What if they say 'Screw the plot! I just want to gather loot, focus on my character build and kick arse in PvP!' Yes, some players will happily set fire to your lovingly woven plot tapestry just to warm their toes.

Enter the Gamer

Let's drop a gamer into E M Forster's definition. The king dies because he was a level boss and the player killed him. The grief-stricken queen vows vengeance and sends the kingdom's entire army against the player, including a whole bunch of mercenaries, barbarians and monster freaks she's managed to hire from 'places unseemly'. The player cuts a bloody path through the nefarious horde and eventually faces the queen herself as the end-of-game boss. She's now a powerful necromancer having sold her soul to some dark god. In a climactic and epic battle, the player kills her and ends up ruling the kingdom.

The king dies because the player killed him. The queen dies because she tried to kill the player out of grief-driven revenge. You see, the story pieces are there, the deaths of both king and queen, but it's the player who forges the plot.

For a fast and gritty education in how players can seriously tear up your plots in favor of stitching their own together, watch *Westworld*, the 2016 TV series. It beautifully divides player types into those that want to play along and those that just want to play. The subplot with William and Logan perfectly characterises these player differences.

William is a natural roleplayer, someone who wants to immerse himself in the romance of story. He wants to be the knight in shining armor. He wants to fall in love. He wants to understand the NPCs and their world. He wants to have relationships. He wants to inhabit the reality of being a cowboy on the wild frontier.

Logan is a power player indulging in his own empowerment fantasies. He wants to have a lot of sex and shoot a bunch of people. He wants to lord it over the NPCs and feel like he is dominating the virtual world, playing by his own rules instead of the prescribed rules of the game.

These player types, the Roleplayer and the Power Player are very real so you need to know which of them will be playing your game the most. If it's William, then plot is an option. If it's Logan, forget about plot and just focus on the mechanics and story context.

Likewise, if you're creating what's traditionally called a 'story-driven' game, then you'll be wanting a writer who is well versed in plot structure. A novelist, screenplay writer or TV storyliner will do nicely here. Look at Telltale Games for instance. Their games are essentially pick-a-path stories. Yes, there are plenty of branches to wrangle, and plenty of 'choices and consequences' to balance, but a branching plotline is still linear. It's just a matter of writing multiple plotlines rather than just one.

The same goes for a game like *Oxenfree*. It's perfectly linear in nature...a bunch of teenagers end up on an island and have to solve a ghostly mystery. One event leads to another in a classic king-dies-queen-dies-of-grief kind of way.

The dialogue in *Oxenfree* is definitely *not* linear. What Alex says to Jonas, Ren, Nona and Clarissa affects those relationships in a myriad of ways. Attitudes change. Characters reveal different parts of their nature and backstory. Yet underneath the plot remains the same. Certain events like the possession of Clarissa by ghosts or the act of stepping into a ghostly triangle into a parallel universe...these have to happen. They're a fixed part of the plot and nothing the player can say or do will change that.

What happens if your game isn't plot-driven? Well, now that's where things get really interesting for a narrative designer like me. And you *definitely* need a narrative designer for work like this, someone who can develop a whole confetti box of story pieces that you can scatter throughout your game in order to make a 'story experience'.

Story experience?

I once heard narrative design likened to theme park design. A park ride might have a story context, a must-have for any haunted house or ghost train ride, and the ticket-holder then explores that context, feels part of that miniature world for a bit.

It's a tough thing to explain in abstract so let's get concrete with one of my favorite ever Indie RPGs. *Darkest Dungeon.*

Being a rogue-like RPG, *Darkest Dungeon* is all about the experience of delving into Lovecraftian realms, surviving by the skin of your teeth and going completely bonkers in the process. There is no 'plot' beyond the usual fare of 'mad overreacher explores where he should not and unearths an ancient evil that then corrupts the entire place'. Sounds like a hundred games, stories and novels already, right? And it would've been no different to the rest had not the creators stopped right there and said, "Plot, shmot! Let's give the player a story-rich experience instead." I'm sure that wasn't their exact words, but the spirit of that statement permeates almost every element of *Darkest Dungeon*.

Darkest Dungeon wrangles its world design, glyphs and dialogue in such a way as to totally wrap the player in story without ever demanding that they follow any sort of plot. As soon as a player follows a plot then their choices are limited. *Darkest Dungeon's* limits are mechanical, not narrative. You can pretty much engage with whichever elements you want, whenever you want, within the confines of what's possible for you at the time. I'm going to go into the specific elements in more depth later on. For now, let's dip our tootsies in this narrative bloodbath so we can get an overall feel for what *Darkest Dungeon* does.

Your progress in *Darkest Dungeon* is defined by character levels, character health (both physical and mental) and how much of the game's hometown you've managed to rebuild and upgrade. In fact, the hamlet itself is as much an RPG character as the adventurers that use it as their base of operations.

For a start, the adventurers themselves are the sort of troubled types you'd find in any Lovecraftian horror.

Houndmaster – "A lawman and his faithful beast. A bond forged by battle and bloodshed."

Leper – "This man understands that adversity and existence are one and the same."

Antiquarian – "She searches where others will not go...and sees what others will not see."

That's all the backstory you get, and that's all the backstory you need in a game like *Darkest Dungeon*. Each adventurer is a lump of clay for the player to mould. Different varieties of clay, yes, with different properties, but with plenty of scope for the player to stamp them with personality and sculpt them with experience.

And where does all of this personality and experience come from? Well, mostly from the horrors the adventurers have to deal with in those antediluvian depths. Frightening monstrosities, eldritch curses, itchy and icky illnesses, and the ever-pervading gloom itself.

Darkest Dungeon needs no character arcs nor ticking plot devices. It has game mechanics! Each adventurer has a stress counter. When that stress counter rises too high, the adventurer in question 'cracks' and develops some rather peculiar psychological maladies. Selfishness, masochism, hopelessness, irrationality and paranoia...this list of afflictions goes on. And the result? The adventurers actually start to behave differently during combat. A 'masochist' will race to the front of the party of their own volition so they can invite the most damage upon themselves. An adventurer who is feeling 'hopeless' may decide to skip their combat turn. A 'fearful' adventurer will shift themselves to the back of the pack whilst ranting in such a terrified manner that it raises everyone else's stress counts. An 'abusive' adventurer will cast aspersions on his party-mates, resulting in ever further increased

9

stress counts.

In a nutshell, or nutcase in this instance, each character's story context is expressed through mechanics and succinct text bubbles. No expensive voice over (apart from that wonderfully creepy narrator), no plot to adhere to, and yet the group dynamics are as clear and complex an expression as one might find in a soap opera.

Rogue-like RPGs are renowned for their procedurally generated environments and MOB encounters. *Darkest Dungeon* is renowned for its procedurally generated story. _ ie, at the end you can narrate a story from what happened)

Nonlinear Thinking

But how do you 'write' for something like that?

For a start, you switch off all the lights in your plot brain except for that one desklamp at the workstation called Department of Cause and Effect. And then you get down to the business of writing tiny scripts, sometimes just one line, that capture specific moments of cause and effect in your game. (N6, 2013)

For instance, let's look at some PC Area Dialogues from *Path of Exile*, the lines that a selected player character will say the first time they enter a new area or perhaps when they kill a Unique Mob or Boss within that area.

The Witch

Killing Hillock:
Too stupid to know he was dead already.

Entering Fellshrine:

Looks like the faithful have gone to that 'better place' of theirs.

Killing Fidelitas:

What a pretty creation!

Entering Act 3, City of Sarn:

A big, dead city. My favorite.

Entering Sewers:

Humanity is gone yet the stink remains.

Entering the Marketplace:

Screams upon screams, as soft as the faintest whisper.

Entering Catacombs:

The 'worthy' like to bury their secrets deep.

Entering Ebony Barracks:

Damnation has no wrath like a witch scorned.

These lines are spread out right across *Path of Exile*, but each is a piece of the jigsaw puzzle that is the Witch's character. We learn about her as a 'person' only when she reacts to elements in the game world, and at these points we also get the chance to add a little more meaning to the environment. We can include scents and stenches that can't otherwise be expressed. We can add insights into cultures that would otherwise have to be explained through tomes, flavor texts and environmental features.

"Damnation has no wrath like a witch scorned."

This is a play on the commonly heard phrase, "Hell hath no fury like a woman scorned." So there's a 'feminine vengeance' energy to it. And it's directed at the Templar baddies who, as patriarchal religious zealots, tend to send witches into 'damnation' upon a burning pyre. Yes, a right lovely bunch, the Templar of Oriath. A 'cross' between Bible Belt evangelists and the Spanish Inquisition.

"The 'worthy' like to bury their secrets deep."

Yes, another potshot at devout Templar hypocrisy.

Each player character in *Path of Exile* has almost one hundred lines of dialogue, tailored as character-informing reactions to the environments and monsters that inhabit them. There are seven PCs to choose from so we have a total of roughly seven hundred lines. That's a lot of tiny little pieces of narrative confetti, but when added together throughout the course of the game, they coagulate into seven fully-formed characters, each with a unique perspective on their journey through Wraeclast and beyond.

Down the road a bit I'll focus exclusively on dialogue and how it functions in very different ways to dialogue in almost any other medium. But for now, let me clarify the narrative design process at work here.

To create a one-hundred-line reaction script like that, we can look at each environment, one by one, and write each line as we go along. It's the same with the Boss-kill dialogues and any other incidentals, like running out of Mana or having a full inventory. Every line is drawn from the context in which it will be said.

Templar PC – "I'm no beast of burden."

In the case of *Path of Exile*, we can show some character development because there's a rough order to the areas that can be entered, and to the bosses that can be slain. If the player progresses through the game 'as expected' then it's possible to even create some form of plot. But 'expected' is not the same as 'predictable' when it comes to player behaviour. Yes, you can exhaustively playtest and peer like a soothsayer into the entrails of your backend stats, but if there's any freedom in your game then players do things in whatever order is more convenient and enjoyable to them.

Some bosses can be avoided rather than slain. Some side areas might not be entered until the player has completed all of the main ones. Quest items might be carried around for several Acts before being handed onto the appropriate NPC. So every line has to make sense in isolation while also fitting together into a whole that feels right for our PC's personality.

And to do this, we snap our neatly linear ruler in twain and rap the halves upon our desk like drumsticks as we focus on what's *really* important.

Theme and Tone

The Duelist

On waking up on the beach:
"Sand and the faint aroma of death. I think I've found my new arena."

On killing Hillock:

"Twice as big, twice as dead."

Entering the Southern Forest:

"Good to feel the sun on my face again."

Entering the Fellshrine Crypt:

"Smells of dust and dead devotions."

On killing Fidelitas:

"I'm not sure if I've just killed a man or squished a bug."

Entering the City of Sarn:

"This must have been a truly glorious city in its day."

Theme = Glory.

An ongoing obsession with achieving and maintaining self-glorification.

Tone = Quick-witted and light-hearted.

Charming and geared towards amusing others.

Once you know the Theme and Tone, you pretty much know how the Duelist is going to react in any given situation. He glorifies the stuff he likes and makes jokes about the stuff he dislikes. And as he gradually realizes the brutality he is inflicting in his quest for glory, and feels the emptiness of glory's attainment, the glorification becomes less enthusiastic and the jokes a little darker.

The Duelist thinks of Wraeclast as a giant arena laid out for his own glorification. Yes, he's a Logan-style character, an in-game embodiment of the Power Player. That's his story, and the player finds that out by simply experiencing their exile in all of its gory glory.

Now, plot isn't completely absent in a game like *Path of Exile*. No matter how mechanically-oriented your game is, it's likely there's still room for a few mini-plots along the way, in the form of 'Quests'.

Quests

RESEARCH AS a SENSE) OF 'QUESTS'

Tarkleigh

Offering the 'Dirty Job' quest (if the player has not seen the Fetid Pool yet):

"Got a job for you, if you're willing. There's a pool near the Mud Flats needs investigating. You'll smell it before you see it. Stinks like a carcass in high summer. But that's not the worst of it.

Dead birds walking. Animals don't rise up again the same as people do here. So if they aren't raising themselves, what's doing it for them? The answer's in that Fetid Pool.

Clear the place out and kill whatever's raising those rhoas. We've got enough living dead to contend with already."

On completing the 'Dirty Job' quest:

"A necromancer? Just the one, was it? Guess the bastard got a bit lonely, decided to make himself some pets.

Well, good to see you don't mind getting your hands good and filthy. Here...to mark a dirty job well done."

A simple plot.

1. We have a problem. Please solve it.
2. Thank you for solving our problem. Here's a reward.

Quests, missions, mini-plots...these can actually provide some quite necessary direction for your players. When 'anything' is possible in your game, it's often difficult for a player to know exactly what they *should* do next. Freedom can feel a little over-whelming at times and you don't want your player to choose to do nothing (log out or switch off) as their default.

Take a game like Runaway's *Splash*. It's essentially a town builder game where you're populating a reef with cute and exotic fishies. To help you in your endeavor, *Splash* offers you a young Turtle NPC to act as both guide and mission-giver.

Feed your fish 5 times.

Title	My First Mission
Intro	(Next dialog after a tutorial step to tap on the turtle to start the mission). T: Ready? Well-fed fish will grow big enough to be released out into the main Reef.
Outro	T: You did it! Here are some Stones so that we can create more baby Angelfish.

Establish the Herald's Angelfish out in the Reef by releasing 5.

Title	Herald of the Reef
Intro	T: We can actually establish colonies of fish out there in the Reef! We just have to release enough of each species.
Outro	T: We've just established our first Angelfish colony. That's so awesome!

Create and hatch the second Angelfish species egg.

Title	Forging Friendships
Intro	T: We can create some new Angelfish! They're the cleaning crew of the reef. They gobble up nasty algae.
Outro	T: Hi, little guy! The Reef's feeling pretty choked up by algae so it's sure going to be happy to see you.

Fill your Sanctuary with 9 species.

Title	Cloud Nine
Intro	T: Think of our sanctuary as a test run for life in the wild! Giving everyone practice at working and living together.
Outro	T: You really are a natural at this! Here are some coins to keep everyone fed and happy.

Quests like these in a town builder game help to focus a player's productivity and provide some necessary 'boxes to tick' so they feel like they're making some real progress. It also allows the player to build a relationship of sorts with the quest giver, forging even more engagement with the game as a whole.

But once again, these are optional quests that the player can complete at *any* time or not at all. That means each quest must come with a self-contained mini-plot that has little or no effect on anything else. If completing one quest unlocks another then sure...go with a little plot progression.

Release 5 Zebra Seahorses.

Title	Break in the Clouds
Intro	T: A thick fog of zooplankton is blocking the sun out on the Northern Reef. We need some seahorses out there, fast!
Outro	T: Great! Those little adventurers will have that zooplankton soup slurped up in no time. Bon appetit, guys!

Hatch two of the second seahorse.

Title	Distress Call
Intro	T: I've just heard from our Northern Reef seahorses. They're drowning in zooplankton! We need to get them some help!
Outro	T: Giraffe Seahorses?! Could they be the cutest little zooplankton munchers ever?

Thrive' the Seahorse Set.

Title	Surviving to Thriving
Intro	T: Our seahorse colonies are doing well out there. Now let's see if we can get them to thrive like before the storm hit.
Outro	T: That seahorse colony is even bigger and busier than before the storm! They're super happy with us!

And that's about as much plot as you may ever need in your game. Just enough to point your player in the right direction, to give them some goals to strive for.

The rest? That's story!

Final Wordies

So I'll wrap this chapter up with a little bit of reassurance. The Plot vs Story thing takes a bit to get your head around, especially if you've been brought up on a diet of linear films, TV, comics and novels. Even nonlinear films like *Pulp Fiction* completely fail to prepare anyone for the challenges of narrative design in video games.

However, it's not as hard as you think when you focus on the simple, moment by moment experiences of cause and effect in your game. This thing happens. This is the reaction. Not all that different from life where we are constantly making up the plot as we go along. How many of our life plans actually go to plan? Pretty much...none, unless you're a total control freak, and then your success rate is likely 50/50, at best.

Every happenstance and reaction can mean one thing on its own and something completely different when you put all of those cause and effect moments together, when you look at the big picture.

I'll leave you with this question about the narrative design needs of your game, whether it's plot you're after or whether story is the better way to go.

Which of these images feels most in keeping with the experience you want your player to have?

A bestselling novel where each turn of the page brings a fresh clue and draws the reader ever deeper into the mystery until all is revealed in the climactic final chapter!

An intricate jigsaw puzzle in which the fascinated puzzler marvels at the beauty of each fragment until finally they step back to gaze upon the completed work with awe and deep satisfaction.

The first is plot, the second is story. The choice, dear Indie, is yours.

3

Characters – Do you need them?

Having written this question I now realize that, not knowing anything about your game, I've pretty much just asked "How long is a piece of string?" My answer to the string question is usually "How thick are their wrists?" or "Have you considered using duct tape instead?"

But you know what? In answer to "Characters – Do you need them?" I'm just going to say "Yes!" and spend the rest of my time explaining myself out of this corner.

So let's try this on for size. If you don't have characters in your game then *your game* is the character.

Looking at a game like *Nightgate*, we could easily assume that there's nothing resembling a character in there. We'd be wrong, of course. In *Nightgate* you're navigating some sort of digital system, trying to dodge its defenses, activate nodes, and dive ever deeper into that matrix until you reach its artificial heart. See...I just said 'heart'. Anything with a heart is alive in some way, and if it's alive, even metaphorically, it has to be a character. Yes, even MOBs are characters, but that's a topic for a different chapter in a different book.

Nightgate's character is the system itself, a cold, meticulous killer. Well, it seems cold and meticulous at the beginning but as you delve deeper you feel its urgency increase, its desperation to stop you. The defenses become more complicated. The parts move with more haste and are increasingly numerous. You can feel the system transform from dispassionate 'swatter-of-a-fly' to a troubled antagonist under threat of likely doom.

Or is this all in our heads? Are we just inventing a character that isn't there? Are we needlessly personifying a bunch of abstract game mechanics?

Probably.

But here's the thing. We humans are so in love with the very concept of 'humanity' that we expect everything else to be human as well. We're like Tom Hanks, stranded on an island, painting a face on a volleyball so that we have someone to talk to. Look at the sheer, mind-bogglingly immense amount of kids stories that turn animals into quasi-humans. Mickey Mouse. Peppa Pig. Peter Rabbit. Winnie the Pooh. Bugs Bunny...and don't even get me started on *Zootopia* or the *Madagascar* series. Then there's *Cars*, *Planes*, Thomas the Tank Engine and Bob the Builder's buddies. The sun and moon both get anthropomorphised on regular occasions. And for thousands of years, humans have been turning forces of nature into people through the fashioning and worship of gods.

A colon, a hyphen and a bracket. Why...it's a human face, of course!

:-)

Your players are going to 'find' a character in your game whether you like it or not. In which case, it's much better if you already know who that character is so you can play to it. Make it a character they can either hate or love. Preferably both.

Now let's look at a game that has a very limited cast of characters, yet has one, single character that permeates through almost every element of the game.

I'm sorry. If you don't want me to spoil *Machine for Pigs* for you then you'd better close your eyes for the next few paragraphs.

Machine for Pigs has a main character, the protagonist, but he's not the *most important* character in the game. The protagonist's sons aren't the major characters either, nor are the nefarious pigmen. The main character in *Machine for Pigs* is the machine itself. And it's a character that is both rational and evil at the same time. In fact, it's evil because of its utter rationality.

The Machine was built with a purpose in mind and it wants to fulfill that purpose. And what is that purpose? Well...it's the biggest steampunk abattoir you've ever seen so what else could it be for but wholesale slaughter?

Sideline...as a vegetarian, I simply couldn't miss the damning critique of the meat industry.

As it turns out, The Machine is pretty much synonymous with the game in *Machine for Pigs*, even to the point where you are pulling levers, busting fuses and generally being a nasty saboteur, specifically to damage and ultimately destroy the Machine. Actually, 'kill' the Machine rather than destroy it, as everything you do in there feels like you're doing it to the inside of something living and breathing...like being inside the body of a giant person.

Yes, there I go, anthropomorphising something that has neither soul nor conscience. But in this case, The Chinese Room, makers of *Machine for Pigs*, have provided the personality for me. The Machine, The Game, The Person are all one and the same. Break the Machine, beat the game, kill the 'bad guy'. Three quite different interpretations of one course of action.

Right, so let's get practical about this. How do you, as an Indie developer, create a pervading 'character' for your game? You start by looking at other Indie games and deciphering their personalities.

The wild west town builder, *1849*, is an honest, hard-working, big-drinking pioneer. No airs and graces, just a weathered, pragmatic soul who wants to turn raw resources into a comfortable living.

The time-based text adventure, *Lifeline*, is a strung-out geek who is feeling thoroughly 'thrown in the deep end' but is nonetheless compelled to press on and survive the scenario with feigned confidence and plenty of complaining.

Oxenfree is a teenager in the 1980s who desperately wants to feel mature and independent but gets reminded of her childishness when the world turns out to be far stranger than her know-it-all self can cope with.

The thing is, once you know what the character of your game is, *who* your game is, then you'll know what sort of relationship you can foster between your game and the player. Is it going to be a friendly, supportive relationship? Is it adversarial? Does your game believe in the spirit of healthy competition or in malevolent delight of control and oppression?

Once you've worked out the sense of character that permeates your game, you can then consider whether or not you need a cast of in-game characters whose function it is to support and challenge the overall character.

This is starting to sound a little confusing to my ears so I'm going to whip up some quick labels for these two very different versions of 'character'.

Macro-Character = The anthropomorphism of your game as a whole. If your game was a person, what would they be like?

Micro-Character = Any character that inhabits your game. Player characters and Non-player characters who are there to support or challenge the Macro-Character.

Let's talk about the most important type of Micro-Character, definitely the trickiest one to get right.

The Player Character

The player character is the in-game character that the player actively controls. It's the main user-interface, the way in which your player interacts with your game world.

List One: Lara Croft. Booker DeWitt. Stanley (Employee
              427). Taki. Geralt.
List Two: The Witch. The Demon Hunter. Jack. The Traveller.
              The Highwayman.

Did you notice the difference between those two types of player character? Don't worry if you didn't. The demarcation is fairly subtle, yet extremely important.

List One consists of fully-formed characters. They have backgrounds, personalities, motivations, established relationships and expected behaviours. They're as set in stone as James Bond or Batman. Yes, they can be reinterpreted, as has happened with both Batman and Lara Croft, but the player is still served a nuanced role to play and some pretty big shoes to fill.

They're what I call a Wysiwyg player character. What you see is what you get. And in most cases, their character arc is controlled by the narrative designer, not by the player. Reactions and moments of character development are built into the narrative of the game.

When you choose to have a Wysiwyg, you're walking a fine line between video games and older media such as film and TV. And the Wysiwyg PC is the type with the least potential for player immersion. Yes, you can roleplay Geralt but there's not much wriggle room there for the player to create their own version of Geralt. I imagine actors have that problem with James Bond. They might want to take the role in some interesting directions that simply aren't allowed by the character. A bisexual or gay James for instance? Briefly implied in *Quantum of Solace* but never confirmed. A female 007? Unthinkable.

On a personal note, I gave up playing *Witcher 3* after about an hour because I simply didn't like Geralt. I know that millions would disagree with me on this point, but I find him to be a bland, cold, fantasy noir stereotype. Booker DeWitt was a totally different kettle of catfish. Far more interesting and relatable to me, but not to everyone. And that's the danger you face when creating a Wysiwyg PC. What if your player simply doesn't like them?

By contrast, List Two is a much squidgier type of player character. In fact, I'm going to call them Squidgies. Why? Because they're more malleable than Wysiwygs. They come with a little bit of background, mostly to explain their class attributes or how they came to be in your game world.

The Shadow is a contract killer who is caught and exiled to Wraeclast. The Highwayman is a bandit-turned-adventurer who has come to the hamlet in search of riches. The Traveller, well she/he *seems* to belong to the culture of this ancient and ruined land you're exploring, and apparently they need to get to that mountain in the distance. That's about all we have.

Squidgies provide starters for a player to work with, a boundary in which to contain their own imagination, but after that it's all up to interpretation and/or character build. Yes, they can still have set-piece dramatic events and moments of pre-designed character development, but these are much fewer and farther between than Wysiwygs. As a result, Squidgies have a much lower barrier to entry for both the developer and the player. They take *much* less effort to create and their flexibility means that they can become what the player wants them to become.

Of course, in addition to your PC, you have the option of creating a cast of characters with which the player can engage. Multiple eggs in multiple baskets, as it were. This can certainly help with player engagement, particularly if you have a Wysiwyg PC. More chances for your player to identify with an in-game character.

Non-Player Characters

Simply put, Non-player characters are any 'sentient being' your player meets during the course of playing your game. They can be fully 3D, like Edwin and Enoch in *A Machine for Pigs*. They could be a disembodied voice-over like the narrators in *The Stanley Parable* or *Dark Meadows*, or a disembodied text box like the 'voice in your head' in *Ring Runner: Flight of the Sages*. Perhaps they're 2D pop-up characters, visual novel-style, like those in *Space Miner: Ore Bust*. Or maybe they're simply character portraits with voice-overs or text boxes, like *Galaxy on Fire 2*.

You know what though? It doesn't actually matter what form they take, as long as they adhere to some vital principles. Vital if you want your NPCs to be any good, that is.

1. Function
2. Humanity
3. Relationships

When I'm talking about the *function* of an NPC, I'm considering their mechanical function, not their narrative function. For instance, is your NPC a Quest Giver or a Lore Giver?

If they're a Quest Giver then they need to be the type who can offer the player in-game missions to complete and have boons available with which to reward the player's efforts. If they're a Lore

Giver then we need to establish that they're a credible source of local wisdom. And there's nothing to stop your NPC from being both a Quest Giver and a Lore Giver, and also a Trading Vendor if you have some sort of in-game economy.

Let's look at Hargan from *Path of Exile*. First off, I'll show you the character profile format I recommend using.

Hargan

Age: Early Fifties

Culture: Oriathan Outlaw

Inspiration: Ray Winstone as Bors the Younger in *King Arthur* (2004)

Profile

Background:

Once a fence and a fixer back in Oriath, Hargan has traded and connived his way to Sarn, where he hopes to scavenge a fortune from the relics of a dead city.

Personality:

Although he doesn't seem like the sharpest dagger in the belt, Hargan is observant, resourceful and shrewd... a real survivor. He's also a bit of an amateur historian, making it his business to learn what he can of Wraeclast's tragic past, if only to better value the pieces he finds.

Current Situation:

Hargan has explored much of Eastern Sarn, always evading rather than battling danger. When it comes to a fight, Hargan will save his own hide, hiring or tricking someone else to dive into the fray in his stead. That said, Hargan's one redeeming trait is loyalty. He does what he can to protect those few he chooses as his friends. To that end, he has become 'Camp Mother' of the ramshackle settlement that houses the exiles of Sarn, sourcing food, planning defenses, and generally providing a little order on the fringe of chaos.

Function:

1. Hargan is a relic dealer, trading in various magic items such as Identify Scrolls, Orbs and Virtue Gems.
2. Hargan offers Side Quests that are usually rewarded with Skill Books.
3. Hargan is a Lore Giver, specialising in the history of Sarn and the Eternal Empire.

And here's the sort of thing Hargan says with regards to his functions.

Offering the 'Platinum Busts' Quest:

"Victario was a poet that ended up leading a rebellion, right under the nose of Emperor Chitus. But here's what *really* interests me. Our wordsmith was quite the talented larcenist as well. Pulled off the heist of the century, in the name of the people, of course. Three finely-crafted platinum busts commissioned by Chitus for his favorite trio of generals.

Victario and his cobbers holed up in the sewers. Now that you have Clarissa's keys, perhaps you'd be inclined to search out those heroic busts for me. I'm sure I could make it worth your while."

If the PC carries the Lioneye, Titucius and Sentari Busts:

"The people's poet could hide his spoils from Chitus, but not from us, eh? I knew you were the exile for the job. I'm sure you've been more than compensated already from Victario's hideaways, but here's a little extra, care of something I found under a dead man's bed. Why? Just because I like you."

Of course, you can't define a NPC by *function* alone. If you do, they end up sounding like a non-sentient robot that spouts info from its databank in response to the questions with no more personality than your average cash machine or Google Maps voice.

I mean, that's what Hargan actually is, a bot who mindlessly regurgitates the answers to a small and set number of questions. But we don't want him to sound like that! That's where *humanity* and *relationships* come in.

Your NPC's humanity is based on the information it divulges that is nonessential in nature. That's techspeak for "He tells you stuff that you don't need to know to play the game."

Stuff like...

Upon meeting Hargan for the first time (as a Duelist):

"Now you're a familiar face! A face what cost me some serious coin at Theopolis Arena. Took you for a privileged pretty boy with a death wish. Bet all I had against you. Then you turned out as dandy with a blade as you were with your wardrobe."

It's the characterful, bonus info that really brings your NPC to 'life'. Because, let's face it, our friends, family and workmates are *constantly* throwing 'bonus' information at us. I may know that my head programmer is also a steampunk LARPer called Lady Veronica Silverspoon, but does that help us get the inventory system up and running? No, but it's damned interesting!

And that's what we humans do. We express our interests, feelings, opinions, likes and dislikes at the drop of a hat. NPCs should be no different. Just because it doesn't directly concern the gameplay, doesn't mean it shouldn't be in the game.

And that's where *relationships* come to the fore. NPC relation-ships are a way of creating an illusion of community within your game. Whether they are part of an asteroid mining operation in *Space Miner: Ore Bust*, a harrowing night of ghosts and teenage angst in *Oxenfree* or a team of misfit adventurers in *Cthulhu Saves the World*, it's this inter-character drama that can make or break a player's immersion in your game.

Relationships

Before I recommend how you might handle your NPC relationships, let me first tell you how *not* to handle them.

Drakensang. Battleheart Legacy. Torchlight 2.

In these games, NPCs seem to have absolutely no awareness of each other even though, most of the time, they exist in the same town or even the *same room*! In *Battleheart Legacy*, the first line-up of NPC mentors literally 'stand in a line', and even then they have nothing to say about each other. They're like commuters on a train or subway. No eye contact. No conversation.

Witcher 2. Secret World. Divinity: Original Sin.

The crime here is not that the NPCs don't talk enough about themselves and others, it's that the characters won't shut up! As you may have noticed in the real world, not every person you meet is chatty. Many are downright taciturn and conversation is like squeezing blood from a stone. If you have a game-world where everyone is standing about, doing nothing much, and are always up for a long chat, then you haven't created an exciting environment. You've created a retirement home.

Here's the sort of thing you can do without breaking the bank of player attention span.

Hargan – About Maramoa:

"She's just so... ample, is our Maramoa. In my mind you'll find no saucier specimen of womanhood. Not in Wraeclast, and I'm hard-pressed to think of anyone back in Oriath either. It's the tattoos and that fancy talk she uses. Intoxicating.

She's a cool one though, but I'm working on that. Bit by bit, day by day, I'll tame her yet."

Hargan makes the odd additional reference to his fellow NPC here and there but the above is how he thinks and feels about her, in a nutshell.

And what does Maramoa think about Hargan?

Maramoa – About Hargan:

Hargan is a man of many claims, and those claims seldom dance harmoniously together. A lie is a death sentence in Ngamakanui, so I was raised a daughter of Truth. Hargan is a son of self-interest. He's no warrior nor spirit-singer; he's a *korangi*. I don't know the right word in Oriathan, but in Karui it means 'he who wins wars with false promises'.

Hargan is casual and chatty, a man used to wheeling and dealing in the streets of Oriath. Maramoa prefers not to mince words and has had a much more formal education and therefore manner of expressing herself. *Neither* are allowed to yack on about everything under the Wraeclastian sun.

There's an Indie game that I think does an exceptionally good job of its NPCs and their relationships, and that's *Space Marshals*.

Space Marshals 1 & 2 feature the same small core cast. Burt the gungho player character, Gavin the dodgy tech guy, Ava the reckless pilot and T.A.M.I. the uptight AI who tries and fails to make everyone act sensibly.

How do we track the dynamics between such contrasting characters? We rustle up a relationship matrix, something to show how the *Space Marshals* characters feel about each other.

This technique works well for small casts. Up to five or six at the most. I generally advise against having big casts of characters for Indie games because both relationship-tracking and dialogue can soon spiral way out of control. Small budget, small cast, and get as much mileage out of your characters as you can.

Space Marshals 1 – Character starting points Read from X to Y				
	Burt	Gavin	Ava	TAMI
Burt	I'm awesome!	Utter blockhead.	This guy is fun to tease.	Unable to be sensible but surprisingly effective.
Gavin	Don't you get tired of me saving you?	How do I get myself into these messes?	A loveable loser.	Tolerable because he's useful, except when he's not.
Ava	She's both funny and deeply unnerving.	The only person I genuinely like around here.	Absolutely nothing wrong with me or my flying!	One day her luck's going to run out.
TAMI	Thanks for the info but I totally know better.	Just because she's smart doesn't mean I have to like ker.	She clearly has a memory stick stuck up her digital butt.	I'm the only one with any brains here.

Space Marshals 2 – Character endpoints Read from X to Y				
	Burt	Gavin	Ava	TAMI
Burt	I'm awesome!	How is this idiot still alive?	A big brother I love to freak out.	If only there was someone else.
Gavin	I've grown fond of rescuing you.	It seems my fate is sealed.	Hapless father figure.	Shows how disappointing humans are.
Ava	I can never tell if she's joking or not.	Kinda the crazy yet loveable daughter I never had.	Still nothing wrong with me or my flying!	Useful yet so annoying!
TAMI	Sure...whatever...shoot stuff, that's all I'm hearing.	I hate it when she's right...all the time.	I ignore her as best I can.	I'm still the only one with any brains here.

As you can see, there isn't a whole lot of character progression there. Overall, there's a growing sense of familiarity and acceptance of each other, or should I say 'glum resignation', but no great changes in the dynamics. No one's fallen in love. No one's done a complete turnaround in character. And you know what? That's perfectly okay in a game like *Space Marshals*.

Why? Don't we want characters who live and grow with the experience of the game? Yes...and no. Here's where a lot of Indies and even AAAs get tripped up. We mistakenly base our sense of character development on what we've seen in TV and films. Sure, shows like *Game of Thrones*, *Westworld* and *Mr Robot* are all about character growth. That's what they live or die on. Games don't have that same reliance on character change and growth. Games have gameplay!

Character Progression, or not

Character development is only needed when the world doesn't change all that much. Sure, Westeros goes through some serious turmoil, yet apart from a few 'magical' elements that arise, the places, the people and their lifestyles remain fundamentally the same. Northerners are still northerners. Southerners are still southerners. Greyjoys love ships. Tyrells love flowers. As you watch a show like *Game of Thrones*, the world starts to feel very familiar. This is even more the case in a show like *Mr Robot* where the world is our world, just a part of it we don't often see. So if the world doesn't change then the characters have to, otherwise you have a very boring TV show.

By contrast, games are mostly about changing the world. Usually that means saving it by slaying every bad guy you come across. Or it could be that you need to clear a passage through the game by solving every single puzzle. Either way, your player is making changes in the world.

So let me ask you this. If you've had a busy day at work, putting out a bunch of fires, metaphorical or literal, do you really want to come home and have a life-changing realization that you want to blow up your apartment, collect the insurance, and become a lone wolf existing on the very fringes of society? No, you probably want a comfortable routine of being greeted by an excited dog, making dinner in a kitchen where you know where everything is, and then putting your feet up whilst having a flick through Facebook on your iPad. Well, that's pretty much how your player feels too once they've finished a chunk of gameplay. They want something familiar, something comfortable, something relaxing.

Within your game world, your NPCs become the familiar, the comfortable and the relaxing. They become the steady and reliable in a world that's being constantly tipped upside down. If that's not the case then you're either making a story-driven game with limited interactivity or you seriously need to rethink your gameplay.

NPCs are there to help your player understand and process the effects they are having on the gameworld. They're the rocks to which your players anchor themselves. Change them or remove them and you're at risk of setting your player adrift...right out of your game.

One last note on 'character', and it's more relevant to RPGs than any other genre. Character Development should never be confused with Character Build unless you specifically want one to affect the other. And if you do, it's much better if Character Build affects Development and not the other way around.

For instance, in *Path of Exile* we tracked ability levels by having the PCs make comments about their increasing power.

The Witch

Level 1	And I thought I'd be a dead woman by now.
Level 2	To learn is to live.
Level 5	I think this Wraeclast will serve.
Level 10	Fate smiles with sharp teeth.
Level 15	I barely recognise myself.
Level 20	The very land learns to heed my demands.
Level 30	I no longer need fear. Destiny has seen to that.

We didn't go as far as to have the PCs comment on specific skill achievements and unique nodes in their skill tree. Maybe we should have? It's an interesting thought, having a character whose personality changes depending on the decisions you make in your character build.

Darkest Dungeon is about the only game I've seen come close to mastering the relationship between Character Build and Character Development. It's a deliberately contained relationship, limited to Afflictions and Virtues, and Quirks, both positive and negative. Afflictions and Virtues alter a PC's behaviour during combat while Quirks are more passive buffs and penalties, and can affect the PC's behaviour during general dungeon exploration or in the Hamlet.

For instance, a PC with a quirk of 'Necromania' has a 40 percent chance of rifling through a rotting corpse if there's one lying about, whether you want them to or not. By contrast, a PC that has the quirk of 'Tippler' will only go to the hamlet's bar to destress, nowhere else. Thankfully, both Afflictions and Quirks can be removed through various treatment options in the hamlet's Sanitorium or through reducing the PC's overall stress count.

So yes, to a greater or lesser degree, *Darkest Dungeon* and *Path of Exile* work with changes in both world and character. Yet the character changes are carefully tracked, labelled, and displayed for the player to see in their UI. This is not the classical character development you see in novels and films. *Star Wars* doesn't give you a running total of Luke Skywalker's 'Force Points' any more than *The Matrix* applies levels to Neo's 'zero to hero' journey. But when your player resides in a game world that is constantly changing, that is perpetually offering the 'effect' to the player's 'cause', then all that change needs to be carefully tracked and explained lest it become completely overwhelming.

So...do you need 'characters'?

I think we've pretty safely established that your game is going to have some sort of character whether you plan it that way or not. It'll have a Macro-Character based on its genre, its mechanics, its art style, its music, and anything else you care to throw into the melting pot.

Micro-Characters, now that's a different story. No, you don't *need* Micro-Characters. You can just have your player work with a one-size-fits-all avatar. Or even a customisable avatar with no established personality of its own. Avatars are avatars in the eyes of we storytellers.

It doesn't take much to tip the balance between 'Avatar' and 'Character' however. Even the simplest thing like a suit of steel plate has 'knight in shining armor' written all over it thanks to our cultural conditioning...depending on our culture, of course. Wrap a scarf around your mouth, look in the mirror, and try not to think 'ninja' or 'bandit' or 'burka' or 'belly dancer'. Cultural character traits are everywhere, and even when you're designing an ubiquitous avatar, you need to be aware of them and how they will be affecting your player's perception of their in-game selves.

And if you think having NPCs might be the way to go, then please be sure about why you're having NPCs.

1. Are they there to guide the player through your game?
2. Do they need to explain certain elements of your game world?
3. Are they a 'safe harbour' in a stormy sea of change?

If you've answered 'no' to all of the above then I'd strongly advise you to reconsider your implementation of NPCs. If you have a character-driven story to tell, then perhaps a TV series, novel or comic are a better way to go. Or perhaps a game that's light on gameplay yet heavy on story, such as a Telltale game, or an interactive movie like *Heavy Rain* or *Beyond: Two Souls*.

But if you want your player to *immerse* themselves in a role that's going to deepen their understanding of the world and themselves then please, be my guest.

A Tale of Two Brothers. *Brothers! A Tale Of 2 sons (2013)*

The Stanley Parable. *(2011)*

A Machine for Pigs.

Submerged. *(2015)*

We need a lot more games like this. More games that know how to draw a player into a role, that recognise the fundamental advantage that games have over other mediums. That the player can *be* the character. That character development and player development are one and the same.

One way or another, the player needs to be the central character. No one summed it up better than the old Fighting Fantasy books of the 1980s.

"YOU are the hero!"

...or heroine. Unless you consider 'hero' to be a gender-neutral term which I generally do because 'heroine' is too often confused with 'heroin'...oh...never mind.

Yes, this blank page is here for you to write on. Please...make notes!

4

World Building

Hmmm...what would it have been like if pre-colonial Māori rode moa, those giant ostrich-type birds that used to live in New Zealand but are now extinct because they were tasty? They do ostrich racing in Australia, so I know it's a 'thing'.

Australia...lots of plains and desert. What if this moa-riding tribe lived out in the vast open spaces, like in Mongolia? Actually, what if they *were* Mongolian, or at least based on Mongolian culture? Nomadic. Ferocious warriors. Raiders and conquerors of the Genghis Khan era, and rather than horses they rode something that's a cross between a giant moa and velociraptor.

Or better than Genghis...Mulan. A legendary warrior woman. What if the culture was a matriarchy, where women were the riders, raiders and warriors, and men stayed home to cook, clean, do the farming and child-rearing? I mean, men are generally physically stronger than women, as a biological standard, Brienne of Tarth aside, so we'd actually be well suited to that sort of domestic drudgery while women, being light and more flexible, would be far more efficiently placed riding ostrich/moa.

Ostrich...moa. Rhoa. Yeah, that's as good a name as any. Rhoa would prefer a light female on their backs rather than some Gregor Clegane bundle of muscle and testosterone. Although I couldn't just make them *purely* Mongolian, that'd be stealing from history. So let's throw in a dash of medieval Japanese, and perhaps a dash of another nomadic culture. How about the Bedouin for some Middle Eastern spice?

Now, what to call them? Mara is the Hindu goddess of death. I've always wanted to go to Marrakech. Change the 'kech' to 'keth', drop the second 'r' and we have...Maraketh!

The Maraketh = A nomadic matriarchy that lives upon the vast plains of Wraeclast. Their warrior women ride upon rhoa, a large flightless bird like an ostrich or a New Zealand moa, but with a tail and scaled skin like a velociraptor. The Maraketh 'look' and main cultural sources are the Medieval Mongolians and Japanese although they are also influenced by the Bedouin in terms of language and the goddesses of the Hindu pantheon in terms of religion.

Reality makes for good fiction

Yes, that's pretty much how it works, at least for fantasy. Gather up everything you know about ancient civilisations, mythology, anthropology, along with every fantasy series you've ever read and/or seen. Throw it into a pot and see what bubbles to the surface.

But note that I put the *real* stuff first? Actual history, re-searched anthropology, existing myths and legends...these should be the core of your fictional world. They are what make your story *feel real* because some of the parts *were* real. Worlds once populated by utterly understandable humans who did utterly understandable human things. Yes, even all those Aztec sacrifices make sense if you take a close look at the motivations behind the brutality.

If the references for your world are purely fictional, drawn from novels, TV, comics, films and, worse yet, other games, then you are in *serious* danger of being derivative. You only need to look at the tropes surrounding orcs, elves and dwarves to see just how bad things can get.

Why do all dwarves have to be fair-skinned, red-headed and speak with a Scottish accent? I know that's not always the case, but that's usually the first image we get. Gimli from *Lord of the Rings*. And has anyone ever asked exactly why orcs have those great tusks sticking out of their lower jaw? Do they serve *any* biological purpose other than making it stupidly hard for them to eat?

There's nothing inherently wrong with playing to convention. But when it comes to delivering high fidelity versions of what players 'expect', down to the red hairs that stray loose from his braid in the breeze and the stupendously expensive big name voice actor, AAA will beat out the Indies every single time. They have the people, time and budget to create lavish fantasy worlds based on comfortable conventions established long ago.

Oh, and I'm only using fantasy as an example here because it's such a well known and accessible genre. Orcs, elves and dwarves are as universal and ubiquitous now as Coca-Cola and McDonald's. Tried and true conventions exist in *every* type of fictional world. Evil corporations in cyberpunk. Space pirates in science fiction. Terrorism in military games. Italian mafia in American crime epics. Mutants and cannibals in post-apocalyptic wastelands.

And there's a reason *why* AAAs rely on comfortable convention. Because they know it sells, and they have to know what sells because they have such a massive investment riding on their game. *Witcher 3* apparently cost USD$81 million to make. If you're putting that kind of cash on the line then you're going to be leaning on every safe-and-sound-guaranteed-to-sell convention that you can find. A big game built on convention is not going to make history, spearhead a new genre, provoke thought or even upset any apple carts. Instead, it'll make bundles of cash.

And as an Indie, if you're in this business to make bundles of cash, I'm afraid you're headed for disappointment. Make a good living whilst calling your own shots? Sure. Buy a superyacht? Probably not. Oh, and if that is your purpose for making games, a superyacht, then please put this book down RIGHT NOW! It's not for you.

Okay, now that we've set the stage here, let's get back to the business of building worlds.

Cheap and cheerful

If you're still at the conceptual stage of your game then I'd strongly recommend choosing a type of world that's going to be inherently cheap to represent. *Hacknet* did this admirably with its expression of computer hacking. It's almost completely devoid of graphics, making it a *much* truer hacking world than you will find in *Deus Ex: Human Revolution* or *Watch Dogs*. Oddly enough, real hackers spend their days peering at code and basic interfaces, not VR landscapes of towering 'data fortresses' or neon, *Tron*-like matrices. *Hacknet* based its game on reality rather than science-fiction convention, and the result is fresh, deeply enjoyable, and relatively cheap to make.

Let's look at another very cheap world to build. The post-apocalyptic text and ASCII landscape of *A Dark Room*. Here's a game that represents a desolate world where ragged survivors have to work *very* hard to build a meagre settlement out of virtually nothing. A bone spear, for instance, is made with just some wood and some teeth. When you finally manage to venture out of the settlement, you are faced with a wasteland populated by other scavengers, soldiers clinging to the vestiges of civilisation, and some nasty, very hungry beasts.

The strengths of *A Dark Room*'s game world are three-fold.

1. White on black text and ASCII reinforces the grim simplicity of survival.

2. Numbers are at the heart of every town builder. How much wood and how many teeth do I need to make a bone spear? *A Dark Room* simply chooses to wear its entrails on its sleeve, proving that mechanics are the secret of enjoyment, not cute Smurfs and pretty mushroom houses.

3. Realism supplies all of the challenges needed in a game like

A *Dark Room*. Just like in the real world, other people are a far greater threat than 'savage beasts', and dehydration and starvation are the greatest threats of all.

So here's the secret sauce, as I understand it. Both *Hacknet* and *A Dark Room* have something in common. They clearly understood the core gameplay experience they wanted the player to have and then built a world specifically to deliver that experience.

Hacknet is about hacking, not exploring majestic virtual worlds. *A Dark Room* is about survival and town-building, not consumerism and addictive eye candy.

Don't build your world before your core mechanics. Mechanics should always come first. Once you know what your true player experience is you'll be pleasantly surprised by just how simple and 'on point' your game world can be.

And you will save a ton of time and money in wasted writing. Which brings me to a pet gripe of mine, and something that you should be very wary about as an Indie developer. *Backstory*.

Backstory, back!

To be brutally honest, story is only useful if it actually ends up in your game. It's only worthy of inclusion if, at some point, your player will actually get to interact with the subject matter. So be very afraid if, when your writer is given the brief for your Indie JRPG, they immediately start working on the Creation Story of your world and a vast cast of gods and goddesses that make up its pantheon. Unless your game is specifically about gods and goddesses and the making of worlds, stop that writer in their tracks.

Writers, by nature, are total lore junkies. Yes, myself included. However, if what we want to write isn't going to end up as a Boss, MOB, Area, form of transport, weapon, puzzle, physics mini-game or anything else within your gameplay scope then it simply isn't worth writing.

Yes, there are many players who care what happened thousands of years ago, at the dawn of creation. Lore discussions proliferate across the internet like daisies in a lawn. But you have to remember what the bulk of that lawn is made up of. Blades. When it comes down to budget considerations, you really have to consider how to get the best bang for your buck. The majority of gamers will only care about what's right in front of their faces, especially if that thing is about to eat that face off.

'Bottoms up' World Building

To avoid a whole lot of overkill in your writing budget, my advice is to build your game world from the bottom up, not the top down. Look at the very first piece of game world that your player is going to land in and start answering questions about it.

What is it called?

Why is it called that?

Why does the place look like this?

Who are those people?

What are their names?

Why do they talk and behave like that?

Why is this place so dangerous/puzzling/delightful?

What happened to make it that way?

What are these creatures that populate this area?

What is their purpose here?

How do these creatures survive?

Why do these creatures want to kill/challenge/obstruct/ hinder the player?

I want you to think like a kid rather than a Professor of Theology. To ask a lot of very mundane, basic questions. Because, guess what, when you dump your player in this strange land for the first time, they'll feel like a kid on their first visit to the 'big city' and those are the questions they'll be asking.

I guess I could call this a 'player-centric' world building technique. You are putting yourself in the shoes of the player, finding out what *they* want to know about your game world. And you can simply do that by tricking your brain with this simple question.

If you were the player, entering your game world for the first time, what would *you* want to know?

So now I'm going to double back to what I was talking about at the beginning of this world building discussion: the rather harebrained and chaotic process of throwing knowledge into a food processor, whizzing it about for a bit, and pouring out something that *hopefully* tastes good.

Actually, this isn't really a 'discussion', is it? Discussion requires that more than one person do the talking, and you're a bit quiet right now to qualify as a talker. You're a very good listener though!

Remembering back to the beginning of this soliloquy, the Maraketh example, let's put the principles I've been talking about into practice. The 4-year-old-who-keeps-asking-why principles.

The World Building Process

Let's say it's the year 2011 and I've just been presented with an old ruin that's going to be the Act 1 Town in *Path of Exile*. Currently, it's called 'the Act 1 Town'.

Let my consciousness stream like a toddler's nose!

What's it called? To me it looks like it was an old watchtower. What were they watching out for? Invaders of some sort. Let's see, who are the closest seafaring people who might want to invade this coast? The Karui. And one of the player characters, the Marauder, is Karui so let's have them involved. And the watchtower was part of a defunct empire so this must have been its southernmost outpost. Who lived here then? Imperial legionaries, I imagine. And since the empire is quite Romanesque, and the Romans had a real thing about eagles, let's call the commander Eagle Eye and make him an awesome archer. Oh, wait, Eagle Eye is too close to Hawkeye the Marvel character. What other animals did the Romans glorify? Lions. Lioneye? Yeah, that works. But why was he called Lioneye? Maybe he had a special eye, an artificial eye. What if he'd replaced one of his eyes with one of the game's virtue gems, in order to provide some supernatural boost to his archery skills? So one of his eyes literally looked like a lion's eye gem, or perhaps he had some sort of decoration sculpted around his eye to *make* it look like a lion's eye, perhaps to impress his men and terrify his enemies. So it's called Lioneye's Watchtower then? No...Lioneye's Watch is catchier, and 'eye' and 'watch' resonate together. But what happened here to turn it into a ruin? I guess it was wrecked at some point by invaders, so Lioneye must have been killed by the Karui. Seems a bit weak to have it just be some outpost that got wasted in an invasion. What if it was personal? Yes, what if the empire attacked the Karui first? What if Lioneye's Watch was the staging post for the imperial conquest of the Karui? Lioneye might have even been put in charge of that conquest which means the Karui would *really* hate him! They'd go after him with everything they had. There would likely be a one-on-one battle between Lioneye and the Karui King...

As you can see, one question leads to an answer which leads to an evaluation of that answer which leads to another question and so on. That's really the guts of the world building process. Start where the player starts, where they are standing on the brink of your world, and ask questions of what you see there. Then just keep asking questions until you run out, until you can't possibly think of anything else to ask.

At that point, take a look around and admire your handiwork, because those questions, one by one, have been the stones from which you've built your castle.

And a bloody strong castle it will be.

5

Story Glyphs – An Introduction

Voice-overs cost an absolute bomb. Here in NZ, you're looking at between $400 and $1000 per hour to hire a studio, a director, and some quality voice actors.

And if you want to create fully rendered cutscenes of the type that Blizzard does, you might as well drop a nuke on your budget!

But you've still got a story to tell, right? Yes you do and yes you must! Players love story because, guess what, they're human. We're wired for story. We look for it in everything. It's how we make sense of the world, so story is how gamers make sense of your game world too.

The problem is that traditional story techniques, the ones pinched from film and television, are so expensive to do properly that only AAAs can sustainably use them. What's a poor Indie to do?

The story glyph. A fragment of story that the player accesses during play. Notes and books, graffiti and hieroglyphics, road signs and 'All Dead Here' warnings, all are story glyphs of one form or another.

Before I delve deeper into this Sea of Extreme Usefulness, I need to clarify something. The term 'story glyph' is something I made up. Having talked with a number of fellow narrative designers about this stuff, the conclusion is that there's no 'international standard' term for this multitude of tiny, gleaming narrative gems. So I had to go ahead and create a name that made sense to me.

A quick history of the Story Glyph

The term came about during my early days at *Path of Exile*, the game where I really learned to wrangle plotless storytelling. We had these seashells that fitted into a cliff face. Once slotted home, they magically drained a pool and allowed access to an area called the 'Submerged Tunnel', a place filled with crabby, crawling things and squiddy creatures hell-bent on eating your face off. Yes, a charming holiday destination.

Someone on the team had called the shells 'glyphs' as a placeholder. A 'glyph' is just a fancy word for a symbol that has a specific meaning. Letters and numbers are glyphs. Logos are glyphs. I simply added the word 'Story' to the front to clarify that these particular glyphs are designed to contain 'story meaning' pertinent to the game they inhabit.

It rolls off the tongue and is as good a name as any, so I've decided to stick with it.

Types of story glyphs

Honestly, story glyphs are legion. No sooner do I try to catalogue them, another type pops up to give me the definitive finger. As a result, I'm pretty vague and squidgy with my story glyph types. For the sake of clarity and simplicity, let's focus on the three most common forms.

Tomes

Flavor Text

Environmental Features

Yes, this blank page is here for you to write on. Please...make notes!

6

Tomes

A 'tome' is any piece of text that can be read in the quiet moments of a game. Yes, they can be read at other times as well, but if a player is forced to absorb a story glyph whilst fending off a small horde of zombies, their comprehension is going to suffer. Have you ever tried to play tennis whilst reading a novel? Ever tried to read a blog post while your toddler daughter is whining that her elder sister has chocolate bits in her half of the cookie and she doesn't?

We had to overcome this problem in *Path of Exile*. Not the chocolate bits in the cookie issue although I'm sure that's happened more than once in the Grinding Gear Games kitchenette. Our first shot at tomes resulted in some Karui carvings situated along the coastline of Act 1. Their purpose was to tell the story of the Karui invasion of the southern coast of Wraeclast and how the Karui abandoned the area later due to some pretty grim and dark happenings. The carvings had pop-up text and worked really well, apart from one thing. While reading them, the player could still be attacked by any passing zombie, sand spitter or rogue scavenger. Being assaulted is not conducive to relaxing reading. What's the domestic equivalent? Um...trying to catch up on your emails whilst your dog humps your leg.

We later rectified this problem, creating 'safe zones' where the player could read these story glyphs in peace. Shavronne's Diary in Axiom Prison, that was the first one. A self-contained area completely devoid of monsters. We carried this tradition on with Izaro's Labyrinth and Daresso's Arena, forging antechambers where the player could soak up the lore in peace before entering the frenzied violence of the area beyond.

A Machine for Pigs takes a different approach. Whenever you click on one of the many single-page documents littered about the game, you are drawn into a full-screen pop-up. The game freezes while you read the various histories of the great machine and the nefarious circumstances under which it was constructed. And these tomes actually serve two purposes.

1. By reading them you gain an understanding of why the world is the way it is and how your actions, as a player, might affect that world.

2. They provide much needed oases in a desert of fear and survival. No survival horror wants their player to get used to being scared. Being used to fear isn't all that different from not being afraid at all. Tomes provide rest periods where stress can subside, making the subsequent tension and anxiety even more palpable. There's a reason why rollercoasters go up and down and not just straight up. Well, gravity is the other one.

Size matters

Now, let's talk about the various shapes and shades these tomes can come in. At their simplest, and worst, they are the hefty, multi-page documents that litter games like *Skyrim*. Verbosely written, high fantasy mini-epics. I believe it's a hangover from early RPGs like *Baldur's Gate* that were graphically simple and slow-paced. Those old RPGs *needed* that kind of heavy reading to help make sense of the gameplay. But in a high-action 3D RPG you're asking a player to study a textbook on medieval history whilst in the thick of the Battle of Hastings. No wonder our eyes glaze over at the mere sight of these dusty works, that is unless we get to hit something with them. From the sheer size and weight of some of those *Skyrim* tomes, we'd do some serious damage too.

A good rule of thumb is this...

"If it can't be said in under 100 words then it's not a story glyph and doesn't belong in a game."

Got stuff you want to share that's bigger than 100 words? That's what complementary story products are for. Short story collections, comics and novels set in your game world. Unless you're writing interactive fiction, don't bury your gameplay under tons of reading. The creators of *Infinity Blade* chose to complement their games brilliantly by having Brandon Sanderson write novellas that link the three *Infinity Blade* games together, giving you all of the story context you could ever want without compromising the in-game experience. The games are *much* better for it.

Tomes can vary depending on your game context. Leather-bound books, scrolls, tattered parchments...these all work well in a fantasy setting. If your game is futuristic, perhaps cyberpunk, then tomes can be digital. Take the myriad of ebooks and emails that you can read in a game like *Deus Ex: Human Revolution*. You need only look around at our present day world to witness the sheer weight of text that surrounds us, from the ingredients list on the back of a muesli bar wrapper to the health notices that festoon a doctor's surgery. Tomes are legion.

Speechless

I know this blasts my previous definition out of the water, but tomes can also be purely visual, like the little illustrations that you can collect in *Submerged*. These illustrations tell the story of how the only two 'human' characters, Miku and Taku, came to find themselves in the flooded ruins of a post-apocalyptic city, Taku injured, Miku fighting to save his life. These tomes also do a good job of explaining how the city was ruined in the first place.

Interestingly, the developers of *Submerged* have freely admitted that their collectable illustrations came about due to budgetary restraints. They were hoping to have cutscenes but simply couldn't afford them, so they settled for cheap and easy illustrations. The result...a far more poignant expression of the backstory than cutscenes could ever achieve.

Too much of a good thing

But be careful about *how many* tomes you have in your game, and what purpose they serve. I mentioned *Human Revolution* before and its many emails and ebooks. Too many. And when you take a closer look at these digital tomes, only a small number are pertinent to what actually happens in the game. Actually, the same can be said of *Baldur's Gate* and *Diablo*. Interesting stuff, but did I really need to know it? The fact that I can't remember any of them is probably 'enough said' on that front.

The best kind of tome does two things.

1. It provides a concrete piece of information that will help the player complete the game.
2. It builds the player's understanding of your game world.

Human Revolution does the former by providing security codes in emails and on the digital notebooks that can be looted from fallen foes. It does the latter by increasing your understanding of important in-game characters like Hugh Darrow. However, *Human Revolution* also delivers an abundance of story glyphs that do neither. Most emails reveal nothing more than the day to day minutiae of people leading near-future lives that differ only slightly from our own. Honestly, you'd have more fun reading the emails in your Spam folder.

Mundane story glyphs are dangerous because they deter a player from reading *any* story glyphs in your game. If 4 out of 5 glyphs are mere trivia then they'll just pass on the whole 'reading thing' in favor of more amusing pastimes like hacking door-codes and blasting baddies without caring a jot as to who they are or what they had for breakfast.

As a side note, unless the player character or someone they know was on the menu, *no one* needs to know what your Bosses and MOBs had for breakfast.

Economical expression

Tomes are an efficient and economical method of delivering story without getting in the way of gameplay. They can provide hints and tips to the player whilst building and deepening their understanding and appreciation of the virtual world you've created for them. But keep them short and sweet, and use them sparingly.

And most of all, make sure they're well written. If you're hiring a writer to produce tomes for you, check to see if they have a background in flash fiction, copywriting for the web, or at least short stories. Don't hire a novelist to write your story glyphs. That will end badly, for everyone. I've seen this happen, sadly more than once.

Tomes as jigsaw pieces

One last note on tomes before we move on. If you have a linear plotline that you want to somehow include in your non-linear game, hack that plotline into pieces and mix them up on your kitchen table. Literally look over your plotline and write every key scene, moment, and idea on a series of cards, and throw those cards down on a table in no particular order. Then turn each of those story fragments into a self contained story glyph.

For instance, if you wanted to make a game out of the first *Alien* movie, you could take the moment where the baby alien bursts out of John Hurt's chest and write it as a post-mortem medical report that the player finds in the medbay. With a bit of creativity, and bashing one's head against a keyboard, any dramatic moment can be converted into a tome that can be read at any time in your game and will still, when combined with other tomes, add up to a complete and horrifying story. Better yet, you save a bundle on art and animation because all the expensive CGI happens inside your player's head.

So lay out those story pieces and let the player solve the narrative jigsaw puzzle for themselves. And in this instance, those pieces can be tomes.

Yes, this blank page is here for you to write on. Please...make notes!

7

Flavor Text

At its most basic, flavor text does what it says on the tin: adds flavor to the items and interactive paraphernalia of your game. Take this tasty morsel found upon grenades in *Far Cry 3: Blood Dragon.*

"Also known as the Island of Spice, this beautiful Caribbean island is a global destination for tourists. Wait, that's Grenada the country. Grenades, on the other hand, explode. You f**king throw them and yell something dumb like "Grenade out!" And then they blow up."

Very droll and it perfectly establishes the pithy attitude of a game like *Blood Dragon*. A brutal satire of FPS games and 80s action movies.

But flavor text can actually do a lot more than simply exude attitude. Like tomes, they can provide gameplay hints whilst also enhancing your player's understanding and emotional investment in your game world.

The Baleful Gem – Path of Exile

"The withering glare of corruption, made corporeal and pellucid in crystal."

If done right, flavor text should be like a Russian doll. Or an onion. Layers, donkey! To see what I mean, let's unwrap that Baleful Gem text.

Firstly, there's a gameplay hint in 'withering'. This gem, when combined with another item, Maligaro's Spike, can be used against the roots of a giant tree that seal the entrance to an ancient ruin. The gem will kill the tree, literally 'wither' it away.

Secondly, there's the reference to 'corruption'. Let's not spoil this one for you as it's one of the 'big reveals' in *Path of Exile*. Suffice to say that corrupting energies permeate the game world. Understanding corruption's effect, and its source, is vital to unravelling the story of Wraeclast, its post-apocalyptic state, and why certain powerful characters are so interested in the place.

Finally, 'made corporeal and pellucid in crystal' is an inference to another gameplay element in *Path of Exile*. Virtue gems. It's a clue to the fundamental nature of virtue gems, how they work and where they come from.

Hopefully this example helps you to see just how powerful flavor text can be as a storytelling device. And maybe this one.

"Ash nazg durbatulûk, ash nazg gimbatul, ash nazg thrakatulûk, agh burzum-ishi krimpatul."

"One Ring to rule them all, One ring to find them; One ring to bring them all and in the darkness bind them."

Yup, flavor text, as a narrative device, has been around for *quite* some time.

Every line should be a riddle that the player can solve, if they put their mind to it. And *players* will strive to work this stuff out. There are whole Reddit threads devoted to the musings and theories of *Path of Exile* players as they debate the meanings of item flavor texts.

Suits of Meaning

Flavor texts need not work in isolation, either. While this is particularly pertinent to item-rich RPGs, any game that features sets of virtual collectables can create something I call 'Suits of Meaning'. At its most literal, this is a suit of armor comprised of boots, greaves, gauntlets, a breastplate and helmet. Let's throw in a ring and a medallion for good measure. And let's also say that this complete kit belonged to a historical figure within the game world.

We'll use a character from *Bloodgate: Age of Alchemy* as an example.

Pyre's Cowl	"All I want to do is bring a little warmth to this land." – Lord Pyre
Pyre's Cuirass	"It's a curious fact that human fat is highly flammable." – Lord Pyre
Pyre's Brassards	"Fire's not the sort of lover you can hold hands with." – Lord Pyre

Pyre's Way	"I've not met a roadblock that a good fire couldn't rectify." – Lord Pyre
Pyre's Light	"No need to fear the dark. I'll light your way." – Lord Pyre
Pyre's Medal	"When the army's away, someone has to keep the homefires burning." – Lord Pyre

Yes, Lord Pyre is a pyromaniac, something that is hinted at in each line, and is overwhelmingly conclusive once all of the lines are put together. Note that he's also an unashamed pyromaniac, convinced that his arsonist ways are somehow justified, even righteous.

Now the player has the option of donning Lord Pyre's armor, and by doing so, wearing the very character of this noble firebug. It's hard not to feel like 'the righteous, cleansing flame' when encased in a suit of meaning like that.

On the flipside, the Lord Pyre set can be used to establish our connoisseur of conflagration as an antagonist, a Level Boss perhaps, one who would be rather miffed to see an imposter strutting about in his beloved kit. In six lines we've established a villain. And as the saying goes, 'Better the devil you know'. Boss kills are so much more satisfying when you actually know the guy you're taking down.

Flavor Texts need not be limited to items either. They can festoon any number of interactive elements in your game. Take warp points on a map. In *Path of Exile*, you can warp into various areas from the Act hub or town. Each warp point has a line or two of flavor text.

Mudflats – "Mud and air seethe with warped life."

The Ship Graveyard – "Whispered agonies of the marooned dead."

Fellshrine Ruins – "The ground aches with desecration. The rain tastes of blight."

These flavor texts add extra layers of atmosphere to an area, layers that can't be done with in-game assets. You can't 'taste' the rain in Wraeclast, nor can you feel 'seething' or 'aching' beneath your feet. Flavors like these supplement the visual and audio expressions of the game with other senses that can't otherwise be expressed in an isometric ARPG made for the PC.

Area flavor texts can also provide historical context to a virtual environment.

Ancient Pyramid – "Two thousand years of regret."

The Docks – "Life pales in the wake of progress."

The Sceptre of God – "The taller the tower, the greater the fall."

These areas are sites of past tragedies. The first and last refer to the fall of empires due to the ambitious follies of their leaders. The middle one is about slavery and the dehumanizing effects of industrialization.

The intention is to create that sense of history one feels when you enter a real-world landmark, like when I walked the cobbled streets of Rome and had the bizarre sense that my sneakered feet were walking on the same stones that had borne the marching sandals of Roman legionaries.

You can even add flavor text to under-the-hood game elements like skill trees. Specific character builds in *Path of Exile* now have names and flavor text.

Ranger Class: Deadeye

"A woman can change the world with a single well-placed arrow."

It reflects both a philosophy about how the game world works and a preferred style of gameplay that favors long-ranged weapons and accuracy over everything else. Meaning and mechanics, working together to deepen the player experience.

But how do you create good flavor texts? How do you forge lines that resonate, that carry a far weightier meaning than their few words would imply?

Hire a poet. Or at least make sure your narrative designer has had some experience in poetry or songwriting.

Sounds cool

And I can tell you one easy way to utterly screw up your flavor texts, and that's to just 'write something that sounds cool'. This is a common trap that many a developer has fallen into, and to be perfectly honest, it's usually because there's a game designer (who writes in their spare time) doing the work. It takes years of practice for a poet to be able to write lines that allude to something large, looming and deeply engaging. A piece of flavor text is the tip of an iceberg and the reader should feel the mass and weight of that iceberg lurking beneath the surface. Writing stuff that 'sounds cool' leads to lines that make no sense upon closer inspection, and after a hundred or so items, flavor texts that all sound pretty much the same.

"The Fist of Az'Turrasq" from Diablo III

'The corrupt magistrate of Az-Turrasq punished petty crime on a whim in the name of order. Innocent and guilty alike were crippled or killed by the hundreds during his terrible reign.'

Well, he's a magistrate, isn't he? How can his punishment of petty crime be whimsical? It's his job! He's paid to do it. And hold on, so if he's supposed to be punishing petty crime, then why are the 'innocent' being crippled and killed? I mean, sure, petty crime doesn't equate to murder or mayhem, but someone who lifts your purse in the marketplace isn't what you'd call 'innocent'. So he can't tell the difference between whimsy and duty, nor can he discern petty crime from innocence. Yup, he surely was a 'terrible' magistrate.

But hey, it's got words like 'corrupt' and 'crippled' and 'terrible reign' so at least it *sounds* cool!

Sounds boring

This is the flipside of the coin. Flavor text that makes perfect sense, offers plenty of logically conceived detail, and is just downright boring.

"Firebird's Eye" from Diablo III

'This orb is nothing less than a super spun energy gyre. Arcane and even thermal energies can be sealed within its eddies for long periods of time and then as the spin is reversed those energies unspool and may be employed.' – Magus Arrin Eberhart

Flavor text isn't about facts. The item stats are there to tell you how that item works. The flavor text is there for...well, flavor. It should evoke a feeling about the item, and about the world it belongs to. And yes, boredom is a feeling, but it's not one you particularly want anyone playing your game to feel.

Sounds like a sales pitch

"Last Breath" from *Diablo III*

> *'Even an immortal could be felled by the power of this blade.'*

Oh yeah? Do I get a free set of steak knives with it?

Dodging the flavorsome pitfalls

So here's one way you can avoid the nonsensical, the samey, the dull, and the salesy pitfalls of flavor text writing.

Theme your items. If you have a set of items that are designed to belong to a particular culture, like the Maraketh from the worldbuilding chapter, then make sure your flavor texts also reflect their culture and style as well as substance. Have a look at ancient Mongolian and Japanese sayings and proverbs. Get a feel for how they are written, what imagery they use, and what spiritual references they tend to make. Then have your writer emulate that style whilst referring to the lifestyles, goddesses, and philosophies that are important to the Maraketh. Use the flavor texts to build the player's understanding of this fictional culture they're encountering.

It's great if flavor texts can refer to specific figures and events in your game lore. You can't go far wrong if you are dealing with characters and historical happenings that have been well thought out and are part of your existing canon.

Thousand Ribbons Robe

> "The night of a thousand ribbons,
>
> To remember the day of a thousand flames,
>
> When Sarn burned,
>
> And was born again."

The above item and flavor text refers to the night that Sarn, the capital of the Eternal Empire in Wraeclast, suffered a fire that destroyed much of the city and killed thousands of people.

Flavor text really can't be rated highly enough in its power to add story to your game, and at minimal cost. You need go no further than 'A Lannister always pays his debts.' to appreciate the sheer weight of meaning that a single sentence can bear.

Golden Rules

So let me leave you with some golden rules for writing flavor text.

1. Flavor text must be consistent with the lore of your game.
2. To help with continuity between flavor texts, have one writer in charge of it. One person who oversees every line, even if multiple writers are producing them.
3. If it doesn't mean anything, if it's just there to sound cool, then don't use it.

4. If it's trying to explain something, it's likely very dull, so don't use it.

5. If it's attempting to sell itself as the bestest, most epic item ever, don't use it.

6. Flavor text is poetry, not prose. Make every word count.

Flavor text is flavorsome. It's there to whet your player's appetite and make them hungry to understand your game world.

Be sure it's on the menu and please make it tasty!

8

Environmental Features

This is a bit of a 'catch all' phrase to cover story glyphs that don't neatly fit into the categories of tomes or flavor text. And the key difference is that environmental features are non-interactive. They're part of the scenery. A player can look or listen but can't 'touch'.

I'm going to hark back to an earlier example I used. The scene where the baby alien bursts out of John Hurt's chest in *Alien*. What if, no matter how much Captain Dallas scrubbed and scrubbed, he simply couldn't get the blood stain out of the upholstery? In 'Alien: The Game', the player could see that blood stain and know that something pretty bad went down there. They can't do anything to the stain. It won't open a secret hatchway if pressed or infect them with some sort of xenomorphic flesh-eating lurgy if touched. It's just there to say, 'someone died here' and that there's danger on this seemingly abandoned starship. Oh, wait, Ripley blew the ship up near the end of the movie. Let's pretend, for our pretend game, that pretty tense pretense didn't happen.

Hints of doom

Submerged uses environmental features in a subtle and clever fashion. The flooded ruins that Miku navigates thrive with ocean life but it's soon apparent that this ocean life is 'wrong' in some way. The whales are the most telling example. At first glance they seem perfectly normal, but closer inspection reveals green algae upon their skin and a ragged, pitted aspect to their head and fins. The whale seems energetic and 'healthy', yet it's clearly been changed by something biological and insidious.

The player who notices these abnormalities in the wildlife is forewarned to the danger that lurks amongst these ruins: infection leading to transformation, a threat that soon manifests in Miku herself.

Similarly effective are the environmental story glyphs in *The Stanley Parable*. Would you go through a door that is completely surrounded by arrows that visually scream 'Go inside!' at you? One of them is even decorated with carnival lights! In this case, the visual feature is backed up by the narrator who is also urging the player to go through the door. But the narrator isn't needed. The door does all the storytelling you need. Someone desperately wants you to go through that door, and that level of desperation seldom spells good news for the person who succumbs to it.

Environmental storytelling is a big part of a game like *Path of Exile*. The mud and blood of Daresso's arena, a snapshot of a Duelist's life, forever killing for the pleasure of the crowds. The fire and lava of Kaom's kingdom, when coupled with towering Karui carvings, represents his fury and narcissistic belief that he is the only son of the war god, Tukohama. Body parts lie around cooking fires and dismembered victims hang from spikes on the Cannibal Coast. Emaciated corpses are piled high in the Lunaris, juxtaposed with the steampunk experimental equipment that has claimed so many in the name of 'science'. Yes, these are pretty grim scenes but that's Wraeclast for you. A land steeped in brutal ambition and tragic hubris, a theme most clearly captured upon the doors of the Sceptre of God where men struggle in a tug of war with the Lovecraftian monstrosity they have harnessed and are striving to enslave. A warning sign that some things are best left alone.

Situational thinking

The thing is, you've got to create environments for your game anyway. Gameplay can't exist in a void unless your game is about an astronaut floating through space, trying to stay alive until she is rescued. Well, even that scenario needs *some* environment. Her space suit. The stars. Other cosmological entities shooting by. So what I'm saying is this...

If you have to create an environment you might as well make one that's meaningful.

The trick is to step out of purely mechanical thinking...this platform goes here and moves at this speed so that it's difficult but not impossible for the player to jump onto...and into what can be called 'situational thinking'.

We're in an ancient catacomb beneath a ruined cathedral. And there's giant spiders. Well, of course there's giant spiders. There's *always* giant spiders, right? The walls are decorated with the bones and skulls of long dead believers. It's an ossuary. So this platform was constructed to allow the monks to transport the sacred remains to various parts of the catacombs. It made their job easier.

But hold on, why is it so hard to get from one platform to another? Weren't these monks trying to make their jobs *less* difficult? Well, time has taken its toll on the great machine that grinds away behind the walls. Everything's out of sync due to rust and bits falling off over the eons. And then there's the curse. These monks, they didn't die peacefully in their beds. Poor monks in video games, they do tend to get a rough deal. Always delving into secrets that end up getting them all killed, usually in gut-wrenchingly horrendous ways.

That's just scratching the surface but hopefully you can see the potential here. Those platforms become part of someone's ancient masterpiece, now masterless and decaying due to the obsessions and follies of the past. The area now has 'narrative weight' that a player will be able to feel when they enter the place. If you've ever been to Salisbury Cathedral or Edinburgh Castle or Alcatraz, you'll know what I mean. You can literally *feel* the history when you walk into these places. It's a palpable weight, not on your shoulders, on your very soul. *That's* the power of environmental features. They can turn your functional series of platforms, corridors, locked doors and traps into something that reeks with historical atmosphere. And when it comes to dungeons, they literally should reek. Unwashed bodies, buckets for defecation, and the mildew...those places must've stunk to high heaven.

Sounds pricey

Of course, for us Indies, there's the question of budget. Bespoke art assets are expensive to make. You need only take a stroll through the flying city of Columbia in *Bioshock Infinite* to see just how much money can be spent on purpose-built art assets. That place is stunningly beautiful and a real testament to the power of environmental features, yet I shudder to think how much money was spent on the thing. Most of it you only ever visit once! Financially horrifying.

Yet there are a couple of tried and true ways that Indies can now create environments that are rich with story yet won't cost the total GDP of a developing nation to create.

Asset stores are a thriving business these days. Of course, the danger with using off-the-shelf assets is that they either come with prescribed meanings or no meaning at all. The latter is more common as asset creators will tend to make one-size-fits-all pieces because they're the ones with the widest appeal. But here's the trick.

Curation

It's not the assets you have that matters, it's how you arrange them.

Let's see if I can give you a more concrete example here. I recently had the pleasure of escorting my partner and young daughters through the *Thunderbirds* studio at Weta Workshop in Wellington, New Zealand. The sets for that show are created in miniature, and to my surprise, they're made predominantly out of 'found' items. The creators scour secondhand stores, refuse centres and online trading sites in search of general detritus they can repurpose and combine into structures like The Hood's ship. Honestly, when you look up close at the thing, it's just a mass of old computer parts, air-conditioning units and any other sort of mechanical 'waste' you can think of. Yet taken as a whole, it's a masterpiece of postmodern engineering.

As an aside, it's an ongoing challenge for the *Thunderbirds* designers to include a classic 60s lemon squeezer in every episode.

This is the kind of ingenuity that's required when building a meaning-rich environment out of stock assets. We're talking juxtaposition and Gestalt here.

Juxtaposition = The meaning formed between two objects when they are placed next to each other.

Gestalt = The whole is greater than the sum of its parts.

Before you dive into your environmental design with all of those freshly purchased assets, have a chat to a museum or art gallery curator. Pick their brains about how they arrange a disparate collection of items into something that has meaning and emotional resonance for the visitor.

MOBs

Although I did say the environmental features are generally non-interactive, your curation efforts shouldn't just concern the rocks, trees, waterfalls and hanging cages containing the skeletons of those who foolishly disagreed with the monarch at the time. Also consider the MOBs. How creatures and baddies congregate, that's just as important as the panels and screens you place in the starship bridge or where you put that blood pool in relation to those mangled corpses.

In the early days we hit this snag in *Path of Exile*. Along the coast we had zombies and hostile humans standing literally side by side. What usually happens when you place a zombie next to a human? Lunch...for the zombie. But in this case the zombies seemed fine with passing up an easy meal in favor of a much more difficult and likely fatal dalliance with the player. Not *every* player will notice these kinds of oxymorons, but for the players that do, their experience of that area is ruined. Tragedy becomes comedy, and if your game is a dark fantasy or survival horror, you *really* don't want that!

I learned a lot from that experience and was able to address the issue in *Bloodgate: Age of Alchemy*. For that game we designed the monsters to exist only in certain environments. Werebears inhabited mountains while werewolves inhabited forests. Fishmen needed to be adjacent to water. Mutant bugs tended to be underground, along with infected miners. We kept a close eye on the juxtapositions of our MOBs in an endeavor to make sense of our in-game population.

Making sense of the world

The key thing to remember, for both landscape elements and MOBs, is that they must have an existence that makes sense in total isolation to the player.

When you go tramping, or hiking for you American types, you should hopefully realize that the wilderness isn't just waiting for you to turn up so it can put on its 'nature show'. For the most part, nature honestly doesn't even notice that you're there, unless it's hungry or you've just stepped in its nest.

Design your environments so that they have their own 'story', a life of their own that makes total sense irrespective of player interference.

This can be done through careful curation of stock assets, bought off-the-shelf, *or* the other way that we'll talk about now.

Bespoke assets

You can always take the 'less is more' approach with your Indie game. So rather than go with all of the bells and whistles of a 3D, hyper-real extravaganza, go for 2D or heavily simplified and stylized 3D.

Amnesia: The Dark Descent and *A Machine for Pigs* are simplified in that they don't have a heap of moving parts to deal with. There are *very* few MOBs in these games so the budget was clearly spent on developing the variety and atmosphere of the environment. Even then you can see that a ton of stuff gets repeated and reused, but the overall effect is of brooding malevolence and that pervading sense that the 'walls are closing in on you'. The situation is similar with *Gone Home*, and even more so with *The Stanley Parable*. Take away the MOB animations and you suddenly have plenty of resources left over for environmental design.

Hey, at the end of the day, I'm a writer. It's not my job to tell you where to spend your art budget. Oh, wait...it actually *is* my job to tell you where to spend your art budget, because being a narrative designer means coming up with the concepts in the first place. So if you want a cheap but effective art style that stands out from the pack and has the ability to tell its own story, the job doesn't start with your artists, the job starts with your narrative designer.

Arguably, that's very much the case with *The Stanley Parable*. From the mundane offices at the beginning to the surreal scenarios 'behind the scenes', every environment is a story environment. In fact, it's even more the case with *The Stanley Parable* because the environments are meant to have been created by the narrator. A Storyteller. You're walking through his imagination, following his lovingly crafted pathways or leaping off them into his half-baked ideas and unfinished constructs. And if you've played *The Stanley Parable*, which every Indie game and narrative designer should, you'll know that even the most thoroughly realized environments in that game are comparatively cheap and easy for a 3D artist to create.

Immersion

When environmental design goes wrong, it often comes down to a very common misconception that immersion is reliant on realism.

How immersive do you find reality? When you step out your door and face the world, whether it be a forest, a suburban street or a parking lot, can you honestly say that you are 100% immersed in that moment? Is your looming apartment building more immersive than a black and white sketch of Gotham City? Is your forest more immersive than the creepy claymation woods in *The Nightmare Before Christmas*? Probably not.

Yet AAA games seem hell-bent on forging 'realism' even in the most fantastical of worlds. But the problem with hyper-reality is that every single detail is provided for the audience. Every hair, every speck of blood and notch on the battleaxe, every fly and every flower petal. The environment ends up so jam-packed with high-res reality that there's absolutely no room left over for human imagination.

And guess what? Short of putting your player in real, mortal peril, like threatening them with a knife in a dark alley, you're not going to get better engagement and immersion than when you spark their imagination.

I'm going to use two gamebooks as my examples here, twin blades with which to skewer your brain like a spit-roast. It won't hurt...much.

Example 1 – Lone Wolf.

I played every single one of the *Lone Wolf* gamebooks as a teenager and twenty-something so I was naturally a bit 'geeky squee' excited when a fancy *Lone Wolf* app was released for iOS. And it was a beautiful thing to behold except for one major and very expensive mishap.

Gamebooks are for text-lovers. You have to be as much a reader as a gamer to enjoy a gamebook. But when it came to the combat system in *Lone Wolf,* all that yummy text and symbolism crossfaded into a 3D, third-person, turn-based battle scene. From black and white to full colour, from imagined to fully realized...in the eyes of the developer.

And the result? A jarring experience that totally destroyed my enjoyment of the gamebook. Why? Because a full bells-and-whistles RPG combat system leaves very little room for imagination. It switched me into a totally different frame of mind, from visualization to reaction, from contemplation to action. When you read, you're on your own clock, pausing to consider what you've read, absorbing the words at your own pace. When you're in a 3D combat system you're on 'dev time', having to react to the game mechanics or die.

Once you've switched from contemplation to survival it's *very* hard to switch back. Impossible for me. My eyes slid off the pages while my fingertips itched for interaction. I switched the game off and never went back.

Lone Wolf suffers from a total clash of styles, and when you have a clash of styles, you have a clash of psychology.

Example 2 – Sorcery!

Back in the day I also owned and played all of Steve Jackson's *Sorcery!* series. Whilst the context is similar to *Lone Wolf*, the execution is like chalk and cheese. *Sorcery!* has both a combat system and a magic system. But where *Lone Wolf* broadsides us with attempted realism, *Sorcery!* welcomes us with the open arms of abstraction. Its combat is represented in 2D, using simple, illustrated versions of player character and enemy. Each move is described in text and the whole thing feels much more like a tabletop RPG experience than it does a video game. Likewise with the magic system. It uses floating letter combinations to construct magic words. Fundamentally symbolic and linguistic.

The difference in overall engagement and enjoyment is remarkable. The transition between reading and combat/magic is seamless. There's no timing urgency with the combat. It's a calm, measured battle, more akin to chess than *Final Fantasy* or *Darkest Dungeon*. At no time was I jolted out of my contemplative, interpretive mindset.

Don't get me wrong. There's still tension and excitement, but mostly because I'm imagining the battle in my head. It's that act of imagination that causes the immersion.

Any room at the inn?

With *Sorcery!*, I felt so comfortable that I was able to lose myself in the story and experience. With *Lone Wolf*, the combat system shoved me into a strange, hostile environment, a situation that made me feel *very* aware of myself.

Whether it be a creation in *Minecraft* or interpretation in *Journey*, the player's immersion is one of imaginism, not realism. Please, build your game environments with this in mind. Immersion is literally 'when you place yourself inside of something', whether it be a pool of water or a poignant visualization. You can't place yourself inside of something that has no room for you.

Curiosity killed the cat...with delight

Okay, so just to hammer this point home one last time....

1. Curation

2. Imagination

Curate your off-the-shelf assets in such a way that every placement of every piece *means* something. Is the Grecian Man statue facing the Grecian Woman statue or are the two statues facing away from each other? Two generic objects, but when it comes to their 'relationship', that's where story lurks.

If you're going bespoke, which unfortunately rhymes with 'I'm broke', forge an economical art style that leaves *plenty* of room for player curiosity, interpretation, and even creativity if your game allows it.

Oh, and get your narrative designer involved in that process from the very beginning. Yes, artists are probably better at visualizing the details of a scene, although not always. You only need to read one of George R R Martin's feast scenes in *Game of Thrones* to understand just how visual and detail-oriented writers can be. But your writer has one advantage that your artist likely does not have. An obsession with story.

Writers see story *everywhere*. They don't buy a mug because it holds the right amount of water or beer. They buy a mug because it has Darth Vader on it and that somehow imbues the glass with 'dark force resonance' thereby making it a magical vessel from which to drink, one that's bound to induce vast epics of dark fantasy prose. Okay, that's *my* mug I'm talking about, and I made the mistake of putting it through the dishwasher so Darth is now missing half of his face.

Half Darth aside, your writer can ensure that your environmental visualization process is steeped in story. Rich narrative that your artist can then mold into stunning eye candy.

Don't get me wrong. I think artists are marvellous people who create pure magic. I certainly can't do what they do. But if you want a game environment that veritably screams with history, meaning and lore, "Don't bring a knife to a gunfight".

Let your narrative designer do the other half of what they're good at: Design.

9

Story Glyphs – Last Orders

Okay, the barkeep is flicking the lights on and off so I guess it's time to shut up about story glyphs. Yet as we sink the dregs of our Pint of Eternal Wisdom, let's recap the basics.

Tomes

Any decent-sized chunk of text that helps tell the 'story' of your game. Books and emails, packing slips for barrels of biotoxin and life stories scrawled on cell walls in blood. They can be found inside ancient libraries, subterranean ruins, abandoned family homes and hackable cyberpunk computer systems. Just don't let them be any more than 100 words long and make sure your narrative designer has experience in flash fiction and/or copywriting.

Flavor Text

All those little bits of poetry, one-line gags and stirring quotes that you find on items, maps, skill trees, vehicles, character profiles and pretty much any other interactive asset in your game. They're perfect for scattering a whole plethora of meaning and lore about the place. Consider flavor text to be your salt and pepper. And for the love of all that's good and just, hire a poet to do your flavor text writing. Please remember that 'cool' is not a substitute for coherent.

Environmental Features

What are you saying about my features? Ruggedly handsome in a chic geek kind of way? Okay...I can live with that. But can you live with player reactions like "It was a bit of fun, and really pretty, but it meant nothing to me". That is most certainly *not* what you want players to be saying about your lovingly created virtual environments. Think juxtaposition and Gestalt. Think curation and imagination. And please get your narrative designer in to help you. They've turned fantasizing into a career so they know a thing or two about visualization and reading between the lines.

Writers see patterns everywhere, much like conspiracy theorists but without the tinfoil on their heads.

10

Hiring a Writer!

Once you've thought through all that narrative stuff we've talked about so far, and how it might apply to the story experience you want to create within your game, it's time to hire a writer.

And where, oh where, do you find such a rare and noble beast?

Start by asking around your Indie game dev community to see who might be lurking about and if other game devs can recommend writers they've worked with.

Or, if you happen to be going along to a game development conference, preferably one of the smaller ones that focuses more on Indies, then check to see who's doing talks on Narrative Design and bowl up to them for a chat. Don't worry, writers are a generally amiable bunch. They're also awesome if you're stuck in any kind of dire, life-threatening situation. Alan Wake, Adrien Brody in *King Kong*, and let's not forget Jessica Fletcher from *Murder She Wrote*!

Failing all that, it's time to hit the interwebs.

Oh, but I mostly certainly *don't* mean sites like Upwork, Freelancer and Peopleperhour. Those places are horrendous 'race to the bottom' wastelands and genuinely experienced and skilled narrative designers will not be hanging out there.

> "If you think it's expensive to hire a professional to do the job, wait until you hire an amateur." – Red Adair

So where *should* you look? LinkedIn, Facebook and good 'ole Google. If a writer has been freelancing for at least a year, chances are they've gotten quite good at promoting themselves online. They should have a website or at least a strong profile on LinkedIn and/or Facebook. It's also worth looking into Reddit, particularly discussions focused on game story and narrative design.

When it comes to keywords for your Google search, go for "senior narrative designer freelance" or "experienced narrative designer freelance". You can also try "game writer" but it's not as commonly used these days. Experienced game writers *should* have "narrative designer" somewhere in their profile or tags.

Please, don't be afraid of hiring a remote-working narrative designer for your game. Most writing work can be completed using a combination of tools like Skype, Slack, Google Docs and Draw.io. Very rarely have I needed to actually go to a client's studio to complete their work. It's nice to have because it's cool to meet who you're working with in the flesh, but it's by no means necessary for the completion of your game.

Yes, time zones can be a bit of a hassle but remote narrative designers make a point of being flexible with their time. As long as you keep your virtual meetings and narrative discussions to a minimum, they're usually happy to get up early or stay up late to accommodate you. I might be projecting my own standards here a bit, but I don't think they're unreasonable. From the remote ND's side, this is a trade-off we're willing to make in return for the freedom of working anytime, anywhere. For instance, I worked full time for my clients for seven weeks out of cafes and hotels in Thailand. If I hadn't bragged to them daily about being in Thailand, because I'm annoying like that, most wouldn't even have noticed. Communication kept flowing and the work got done.

But how do you know if you have the right narrative designer once you've found them? Two main reasons.

1. They should be able to provide you with a sample of their narrative design work. Ask for examples of game development documents as well as scripts and in-game text because your ND needs to be just as good at expressing concepts to your team as they are at expressing story to your audience.

2. Freelance NDs will often give you up to one hour free as a consult. Take them up on that. It's worth it to see if you have 'creative chemistry'. Yet do make sure you're both on the same page regarding what's pro bono and what's paid work. This avoids nasty surprises on both sides.

How much?!

I imagine you're now wondering how much this freelance narrative designer is going to cost you. For a start, there's not much point in asking for an hourly rate because that can be both terrifying and utterly misleading. Different writers work at different speeds on different projects. One writer might be able to knock out a fantastic dialogue script in a couple of hours yet may labour over the finer details of design docs for days, ensuring that there's no ludonarrative dissonance in your game. In my experience, a results-based approach is best.

For instance, if you want a script that lays out NPC dialogue and 'narrative experiences' for about 30-45 minutes of gameplay, you're looking at anything up to USD$1500. Bearing in mind, that's for a relatively linear game with limited narrative interactivity. Once you start adding in branching plot-lines and dynamic conversations, that cost climbs quite quickly.

For Item Flavor Texts or 1-2 sentence mission statements for something like a town builder game, you could expect to pay about USD$100 per half dozen.

A character profile...also about USD$100, perhaps a bit more. Simple quest design and description plus NPC dialogue for an RPG? Up to USD$300.

I have to stress that these are just rough figures that may have absolutely no relevance to what your game actually needs. It's really up to you and your narrative designer to hash out the details between you so that you get a story package that is both effective and *cost* effective.

The thing is, there's no 'by word' or 'by page' values here. Rumor has it that Japanese visual novel writers are often paid by the word, which is clearly why some visual novels end up being 800,000 words long!

It's all about what works best for your game. A single scrawled message on a wall may be far more effective than a 100-word tome. But the shorter the piece, the harder it is to write, so the graffiti and the tome might actually take about the same time and effort to create.

> "If I had more time, I would have written a shorter letter." – Blaise Pascal

So rather than thinking of story in quantitative terms, think of its value in terms of the *effect* you want that piece of story to have. Does it need to provide information about a quest? Does it need to share some lore? Is it about building a relationship between the PC and an NPC? Does it need to do all three of those things at once? If you explain the experience you want to create with this narrative bite, your writer will be more able to tell you how it might be done and how much it'll cost.

Try not to talk in terms of how much. Try sticking with *how*.

"Winter is coming."

Quantity = 3 words.

Value = Incalculable.

I could go on to talk about contracts and NDAs and all that malarky, but since I'm not a lawyer, I'd best keep my mouth shut on those topics. That said...since I can't help myself...trust goes a long way with professional narrative designers. And word also gets around pretty fast regarding NDs with big mouths or short memories when it comes to deadlines and delivery. I wish I could say that everyone was efficient and reliable all the time, but we're humans, not the robots that will soon replace us.

Yes, this blank page is here for you to write on. Please...make notes!

11

What's your story?

That's still very much up to you. So is how you're going to tell that story once you've tagged and bagged it.

But here's what I hope we've achieved together. If nothing else, I sincerely hope that you understand what's possible, and often more importantly, what's *not* possible for your game story. That's what being an Indie is all about. Knowing your limits and then working within those limits to make something truly remarkable.

You see, unbounded creativity is utterly terrifying and for a very good reason. You only need to watch *Synedoche, New York* to see just how disastrous and ultimately fatal the combination of an open mind and open chequebook can be. People go voyaging into the realms of fantasy and dreams, never to return. Others spend small fortunes on creative consultations and concept artists when they should've spent a fraction of that money training *themselves* to develop and express their own ideas.

That's the thing to remember. It's *your* idea and no one is ever going to know that idea like you do. If you get others in too early, before you've done everything you can do to develop it first, there's a risk that your well-meaning professionals will turn your idea into their idea.

Of course, that's not always a bad thing. There's a very good reason why *The Empire Strikes Back* is the best movie of the 'first six'. It was neither written nor directed by George Lucas. Then again, if he'd relinquished creative control of the original *Star Wars* movie, the franchise may never have happened and the world would be a sadder place for it.

There's a time to go it alone and there's a time to call in the cavalry. I sincerely hope you've read this book during the former stage and not the latter. At the beginning, a game concept is like a single flower that's just bloomed. A fully developed game concept is a vast field of flowers, Heidi-style, blanketing an entire mountain pasture. Cavalries tend to trample things when they charge in. A field of flowers can survive that. A single flower...not so much.

So take stock for a moment. What do you have at your disposal? You, a computer, and a few savings left over from that soul-grinding job you've finally had the guts to quit. Or perhaps you still have that job but the mortgage and family life eats up most of the earnings. Either way, your resources are severely limited. Don't worry, you're not alone. *Every* Indie feels your pain, especially at the beginning of their career.

It's the financial limits that separate we Indies from the AAA crowd. And it's those same limits that force the Indie to be far more creative than most AAAs ever dare to be. When you don't have money to throw at a project, you have to throw a couple of far more precious things.

Thought and time.

It's easy to forget the 'meaning' of money but few can forget the sheer gruelling effort of creative thought and that oh-so-finite time we've invested into our beloved game project. Time made even more valuable by the fact that it's often been cribbed away from earning money, caring for family and pets, staying healthy, wrangling relationships, and everything else that makes up the slimy coleslaw of human existence.

So here's hoping this Big Mac's worth of advice and dubious wisdom has helped you realize what's possible within this rather tight squeeze of a sandpit.

Yes, you can still tell a story. You don't have to be a AAA to tell a *good* story either. And in my humble opinion, there's nothing like a massive budget, market considerations and a 'writing by consensus' culture to totally mess up a narrative.

What it comes down to is knowing *how* to tell a good story within the confines of Indie development. It's my heartfelt wish that this book has pointed you in the right direction, that it's helped you not only work out the type of story you want to tell within your game, but also shown you some achievable ways to make that story happen.

Six years ago, I knew pretty much nothing about Game Story. Fifteen years ago, I knew pretty much nothing about Story. Yes, I've taken some courses and read a lot of books, but most of my learning, most of my realizations have come from the investment of those two precious resources.

Thought and time.

Being an Indie is about learning first, creating second, and spending money as a last resort. Thank you for spending your money on this book. May every dollar you've spent here be saved a hundred times over when it comes time to tell your Game Story.

I really look forward to playing your game.

About Edwin McRae

Edwin is a professional game writer who lives in New Zealand and has worked on everything from epic RPGs to town builders featuring cute fish and chaotic goblins. He's also an interactive fiction writer and an author of LitRPG novels.

For more information and news about interactive narratives and storytelling in video games, come and see Edwin's website where he's regularly adding articles about narrative design, video games and the constantly evolving face of 21st Century storytelling.

www.edmcrae.com

Yes, this blank page is here for you to write on. Please...make notes!